Kirby Puckett's
Baseball
Games

Kirby Puckett's Baseball Games

By Kirby Puckett and Andrew Gutelle

Illustrated by Paul Meisel

WORKMAN PUBLISHING • NEW YORK

PHOTO CREDITS

Header: Focus on Sports. Cover: Focus on Sports/Stephen Green
Pages 1, 6, 50, 55, 67, 93: Focus on Sports
Pages vii, 2, 11, 12, 16, 20, 26, 28, 29, 46, 47, 63, 84, 92: © Tom DiPace
Pages 38, 68, 85: AP/Wide World Photos
Back Cover: © Tom DiPace

Library of Congress Cataloging-in-Publication Data
Puckett, Kirby
Kirby Puckett's baseball games/by Kirby Puckett and Andrew Gutelle; illustrated by Paul Meisel.
p. cm.
Summary: Games, advice, and tips for developing the four baseball skills of hitting, running, catching, and throwing.
ISBN 0-7611-0155-1
1 Baseball—Juvenile literature. (1. Baseball.) I. Gutelle, Andrew. II. Meisel, Paul, ill. III. Title.
GV867.5.P83 1996   96—10192
796.357—dc20   CIP   AC

Workman books are available at special discounts when purchased in bulk for premiums and sales promotions as well as for
fund-raising or educational use. Special editions or book excerpts can also be created to specification.
For details, contact the Special Sales Director at the address below.

Workman Publishing Company, Inc.
708 Broadway, New York, NY 10003

Major League Baseball trademarks and copyrights used with permission from
Major League Baseball Properties, Inc.

Package and cover design by Lisa Hollander
Book design by Lisa Hollander with Janet Vicario

Manufactured in the United States of America

10 9 8 7 6 5 4 3 2 1

To Catherine, Kirby Jr.,
and all kids everywhere.

—K.P.

To Sena, Chloe, and Sam,
my all-time favorite home team.
Also to my father,
who took me to Yankee Stadium
the day Roger Maris hit #61.

—A.G.

To Peter, Alex, and Andrew,
who love this game as much as I do.

—P.M.

ACKNOWLEDGMENTS

Thanks to Peter Workman, Paul Hanson, Lisa Hollander, Janet Vicario, and the entire lineup at Workman Publishing, for their help in producing a book with plenty of hits and runs, but no errors.

Also thanks to Ron Shapiro and Michael Maas, good agents and good people.

A special tip of our caps to editor Anne Kostick, for her good judgment and support from the first pitch to the final out.

KIRBY PUCKETT

Kirby Puckett is one of the most enthusiastic and talented baseball players of his time. He started off his major-league career in 1984 by stroking four hits in his very first game with the Minnesota Twins. Kirby quickly became a key player in the Twins lineup and an almost permanent member of the All-Star team. A lifetime .300 hitter and a Gold Glove outfielder, Kirby's incredible, above-the-fence, centerfield catch and his extra-inning homer helped clinch the 1991 World Series for the Twins.

Contents

ON THE BASES

3

PLAYING THE FIELD
4

FLIPS AND FASTBALLS
5

LAST LICKS

6

Foreword

A NOTE TO PARENTS:

This book is filled with games for children who love to play, along with advice and tips to help them play better. While having fun, they can develop many of the skills they need to play baseball. The games have been organized by the four basic baseball skills; hitting, running, catching, and throwing. Since most kids can't wait to swing a bat, hitting games come first. However, younger children may do better starting with some simple throwing or running games.

You will recognize many classic games here. Some have been modified to better suit young children. You may find that the rules need to be adjusted to fit the skills level or temperament of the players. or even the shape of the playing field itself. Don't be afraid to experiment. That can lead to great new games, and great new players.

*"**H**ey, you wanna play?"* When I was a kid, I must have said that a thousand times. Every Saturday morning I would get up, eat breakfast, grab my ball and glove, and go outside. Sometimes I would throw the ball against the wall for two hours before anyone else showed up. But when somebody finally did I always said the same thing: "Hey, you wanna play?" Believe me, this game isn't as hard as it looks. You throw the ball and you catch it. You hit the ball and you run. That's all you have to do. So grab your baseball, go outside, and get started!*

Play Ball!

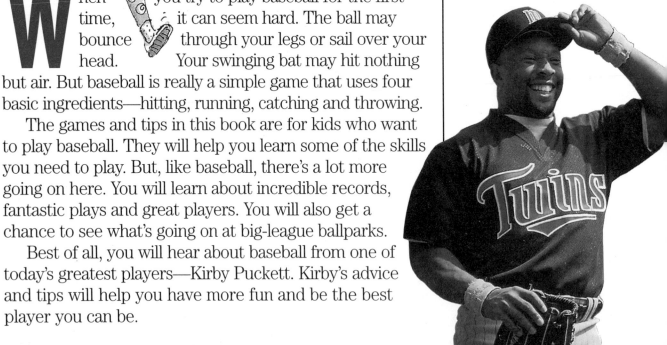

"*I* don't know why, but ever since I can remember I've loved baseball. I was probably about five years old when I started playing. By the time I was eight or nine, that was all I wanted to do. I used to carry my ball, bat and glove to school every day. During recess my friends and I would play in the school yard. I just loved playing baseball!"

When you try to play baseball for the first time, it can seem hard. The ball may bounce through your legs or sail over your head. Your swinging bat may hit nothing but air. But baseball is really a simple game that uses four basic ingredients—hitting, running, catching and throwing.

The games and tips in this book are for kids who want to play baseball. They will help you learn some of the skills you need to play. But, like baseball, there's a lot more going on here. You will learn about incredible records, fantastic plays and great players. You will also get a chance to see what's going on at big-league ballparks.

Best of all, you will hear about baseball from one of today's greatest players—Kirby Puckett. Kirby's advice and tips will help you have more fun and be the best player you can be.

RATING THE GAMES

In the rest of this book there are lots of games to try. Here's one way to help decide if a certain game is right for you:

⚾ = **Rookie.** This is a good game for kids who have never played baseball before.

⚾⚾ = **Pro.** These games take a little bit of baseball skill right from the start.

⚾⚾⚾ = **All-Star.** These games might be best for more experienced players.

BASEBALL TOOLS

Here are the things you need to play baseball:
Of course, a ball is a must. Take good care of it. If it bounces away and you can't get it back, the game is over!

It's nice to have a few bats, but all the players on both teams can share one.

Four bases are placed evenly to make a diamond shape. If you don't have real bases, try pieces of cardboard or towels, or draw a square outline on the ground with a stick.

Most players like to use their own glove, but you can often share one with a player on the other team.

If you are playing with a hardball, you must use a helmet when you are batting. It will protect your head, so you can concentrate on hitting—instead of being hit!

Helmet

Home Plate

bases

bat

glove

ball

BASEBALL RULES

Just in case you're playing baseball for the first time, here's most of what you need to know:

A baseball game is a contest between two teams with nine players on each side. The teams play on a field that has four bases evenly spread out. They are *first base, second base, third base* and *home plate*.

One team takes the field. The other team is *up*, meaning the players take turns hitting. When someone hits the ball, he runs to first base. If the ball is caught before it bounces, he is *out*. He is also out if a player throws the ball to first base before he gets there, or if he is tagged by the player holding the ball. Otherwise, he's *safe*.

Players keep hitting and running from one base to the next. A player who gets all the way to home plate scores one *run* for his team. The team keeps hitting until the players make three outs. Then they take the field and the other team is up.

A game is divided into sections called *innings*. Each team gets three outs per inning. A game usually lasts for nine innings. At the end of the game the team with the most runs is the winner.

THE PUCKETT PRACTICE BALL

Place your first and second fingers on or along the spots marked for the right or left hand. Now slide your thumb into the thumb spot of the same color. You're ready to throw! (For more about throwing and pitching, see page 66.)

GROUND RULES

Managers and umpires gather at home plate before each game. They exchange lineup cards and they also review ground rules. The distance around the bases is always the same, but in other ways ballparks are different. They may have high walls or low fences, a big outfield or a little one. They can even be indoors or outdoors. Ground rules tell what happens when special situations come up in a game. For instance, what happens if a ball hits the roof and falls back on the playing field? How about when it

BASEBALL TALK

BALL *A pitch that crosses home plate out of the strike zone without the batter swinging.*

DOUBLE *A base hit on which the batter makes it to second base.*

ERROR *A play in which a fielder drops the ball or throws it wildly,* allowing a runner to get to a base.

HOME RUN *A fly ball that goes over the outfield boundary in fair territory. The batter gets to circle all the bases.*

SINGLE *A base hit on which the batter makes it safely to first base* and stays there.

STRIKE *A pitched ball that the batter swings at and misses, or one that crosses home plate in the strike zone.*

STRIKEOUT *A kind of out, when a batter makes three strikes without hitting the ball.*

TRIPLE *A base hit on which the batter makes it to third base.*

WALK *After four pitches, that are called balls, are thrown to one batter, the batter walks—or jogs—to first base.*

gets stuck behind the ivy growing on an outfield wall?

You will need ground rules of your own. What happens if you're in the middle of a game and the ball rolls down the sewer? How about if someone hits it into your neighbor's yard? Work out your ground rules for a particular place in advance. Then you can use them every time you play there.

Diamond Dimensions: A big-league infield is 90 feet from one base to the next. If you play on a kid-size field in the park, the distance is 60 feet. If you need to measure your own field, always begin at home plate. Start walking toward "first base." Walk with a nice, easy motion. Stop after taking 50 normal-size steps. Mark that spot and then do the same thing from first to second base and from second to third base.

Borders and Bounds: Some games aren't played on a baseball field. For games like tag it's helpful to mark off a wide open space. You can sometimes set up the game between natural borders such as sidewalks and paths. Or, if that's not possible, prop four sticks upright in the corners of the field. When you get near one side, you can look left and right to see if you're "in bounds."

"**W**e had simple ground rules near the apartment building where I grew up. If you hit the buildings on a fly, it was a home run. I hit home runs—and broken windows! My mom and dad set the ground rules for those. They paid for the windows, and I had to pay them back!"

THE BASEBALL FIELD

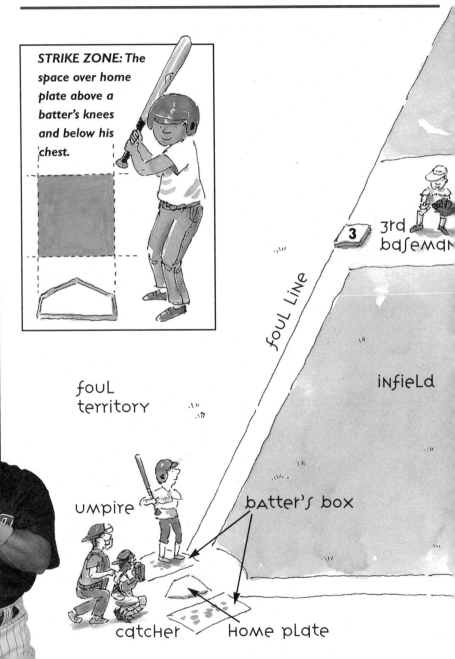

STRIKE ZONE: The space over home plate above a batter's knees and below his chest.

foul territory

3rd baseman

foul line

infield

umpire

batter's box

catcher

Home plate

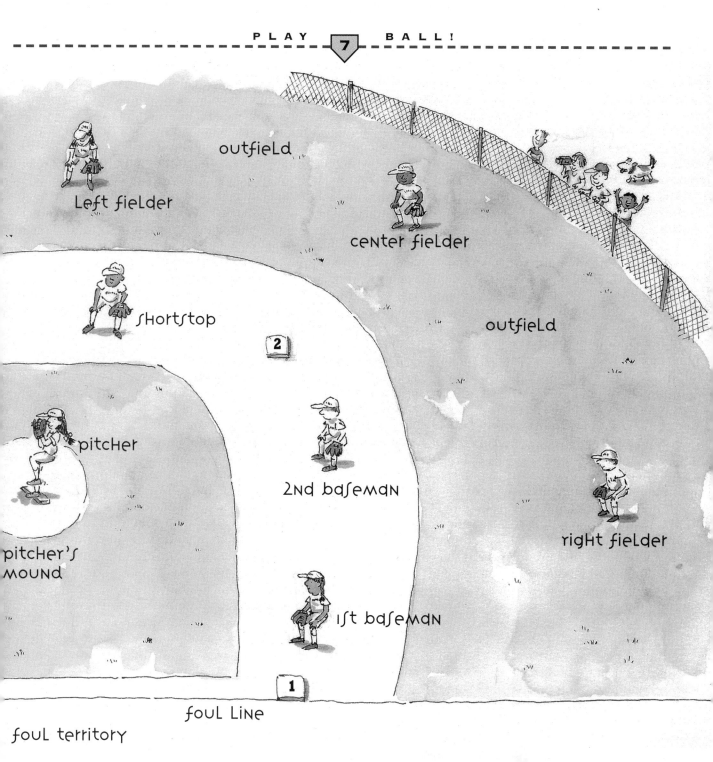

GET LOOSE!

*" **L**ong before the first pitch is thrown, I'm at the ballpark and in my uniform. I always want to be sure I'll do the best I can, so I take the time I need to be prepared. I get my body ready. Then when the game starts, I'm ready to go!"*

Before a big-league game, baseball players take the field to stretch, run and warm up their muscles. Here are a few easy exercise games to get your muscles moving.

Swat the Mosquito: Imagine there is an annoying mosquito buzzing around you. When it is just above your head, jump up and clap hard with your hands. Now jump and swat 24 more mosquitoes.

Home Run Harry: Pretend you are Home Run Harry, the greatest slugger of all time. Stand at home plate and watch a make-believe ball sail out of the ballpark. Now trot around the bases. Pump your fist in the air. Wave to the imaginary fans in the stands. Take a bow as you cross home plate. Now hit four more home runs and trot around the bases after each one. Run a little bit faster each time.

Follow the Base Runner: Play a game of "Follow the Leader." Hop from home plate to first base. Run backwards to second. Walk like a duck to third. Sing "Take Me Out to the Ball Game" as you go from third to home. Make up your own silly moves between bases and watch your friends follow your lead.

*"**S**ometimes you may be one of the last players picked on a team. Don't let it get you down. You need to play with and against people who are better than you. That can be frustrating, but it's the only way you will get better."*

CHOOSING UP

Here are two ways to decide who will play on each side:

Count Off: Line up in order. You could line up using first names from A to Z, or by birthdays from January to December, or by height from shortest to tallest. Go down the line counting "one, two, one, two," from the beginning to the end. The "ones" become one team and the "twos" are the other team.

Pick Captains: Sometimes two players can be the ones to choose up sides. If the two best players are the captains, you know both teams will be balanced from the start, but any pair of equally matched players can do the picking.

WHO GOES FIRST?

Once you have your teams, you must decide which one starts the game.

Grab a Bat: One captain grabs a bat in the middle with the handle pointing up. The other grabs the bat just above her hand. The fists should touch without overlapping. Fist over fist, the two players move their hands up the bat. Whoever's hand covers the knob at the end of the bat is the winner: Her team goes first.

Mystery Hand: Pick up a pebble and put your hands behind your back. Slip the pebble into one of them. Make a fist with each hand. Now hold your fists in front of you. Your opponent picks a fist. If he picks the one with the pebble in it, his team goes first.

PICKING "IT"

In some games one person must face a particular challenge. That's the person who is IT. Since no one ever wants to be IT, here are two ways to choose that person:

Not IT!: This is the quickest way to choose IT. As soon as you decide to play a game, everyone starts shouting, "Not IT!" The unlucky person who says it last is IT.

Short Stick: Find several sticks or blades of grass, one for each player. One must be clearly shorter than all the others. Hold them in your fist so you cannot tell a long one from a short one. Each player picks a stick and you get the one that is left in your fist. Whoever picks the shortest stick is IT.

LAST LICKS

Baseball is a very fair game. The team that starts in the field gets the last turn at bat. That way both teams get the same number of chances to hit the ball, score runs and win. Many other games should be played this way. The team or the player that goes last gets one final turn. So if you don't get to go first, don't worry. You still get last licks.

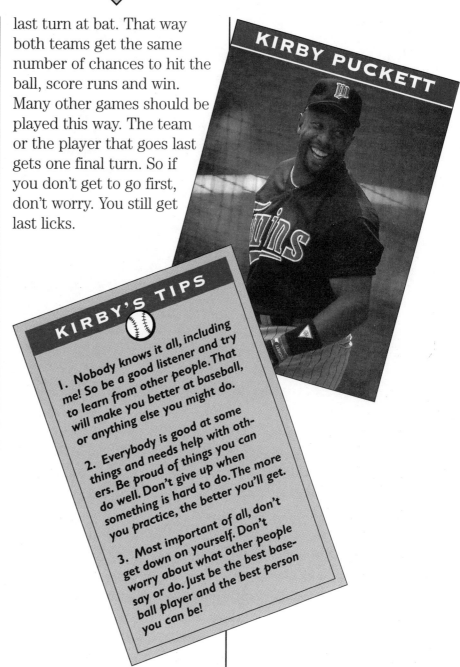

KIRBY PUCKETT

KIRBY'S TIPS

1. Nobody knows it all, including me! So be a good listener and try to learn from other people. That will make you better at baseball, or anything else you might do.

2. Everybody is good at some things and needs help with others. Be proud of things you can do well. Don't give up when something is hard to do. The more you practice, the better you'll get.

3. Most important of all, don't get down on yourself. Don't worry about what other people say or do. Just be the best baseball player and the best person you can be!

Batter Up!

"The way I approach hitting is very simple. Before I bat, I have an idea about what I want to do. And once I step into the batter's box I'm ready to go. I've always been a free swinger. The pitcher can throw the ball high, low, fast, slow, inside or outside. It doesn't matter to me—if I can put my bat on it, I'm swinging!"

Once you've warmed up, it's time to start swinging. Baseball players only get a few chances to hit during a game. That's why it's so important to make every turn at bat—and every swing—count.

Batting is probably the hardest thing a baseball player has to do. To see why, lay a baseball bat on the ground. Now see if you can balance a baseball on the top of it. Getting a round ball to balance on a round bat is almost impossible. There is only a tiny spot where ball and bat touch each other. In less than a second a hitter's bat must connect with a speeding, spinning baseball at the perfect spot. Great hitters must think as fast as they swing.

BASEBALL TALK

AT-BAT *A player's turn at hitting.*

BATTING AVERAGE *A way to measure a hitter's success. Divide the number of hits a batter gets by the number of at-bats he has had.*

BATTING ORDER *Also called lineup. Players on a team take their turns at bat in the same order during every inning.*

9 at-bats = .333 / 3 hits

CHOKE UP *To move both hands up an inch or two on the handle of the bat.*

THE COUNT *The number of balls and strikes called on a batter at any time. For example, a count of 3 and 2 means 3 balls and 2 strikes; a "full count."*

FOUL BALL *A batted ball that does not land in fair territory.*

FOUL TIP *A pitched ball barely nicked by the batter's swing. (It usually goes backwards.)*

ON-DECK CIRCLE *An area near home plate where the next batter waits for his turn to bat. He usually warms up by swinging.*

PINCH HITTER *A player who bats in place of a teammate.*

RBI *Stands for "run batted in." A hitter gets credit for an RBI when his batted ball allows a runner to score.*

PICKING THE PERFECT BAT

In the big leagues, players use wooden bats. You may choose a bat of either wood or aluminum. Make sure the handle is thin enough so your hands fit around it. The bat should feel comfortable when you hold it.

■ Hold the bat in front of you in one hand, so your arm and the bat form a straight line. Now count backwards from 10 to 0. Does the bat start to droop? If it does, try to find a lighter one.

■ If your bat is made of wood, hold the fat end in your hand. Tap the other end gently but firmly on the sidewalk. If your hand feels as if it's shaking or vibrating, the bat might be cracked. If it is, don't use it. Find another one.

■ Run your fingers over the bat. Look for nicks or chips. Try to choose a bat that feels as smooth as the day it was made.

TEE FOR YOU: When you are first learning to hit, a batting tee comes in handy. You can set a ball on the tee and hit it. This is much easier than hitting a ball that is pitched to you.

GET A GRIP

Grab your bat with both hands, making sure they are together at the bottom. If you are a righty, your right hand goes above the left. For lefties, the left hand goes above. Most players hold a bat so the knuckles on both hands form a straight line.

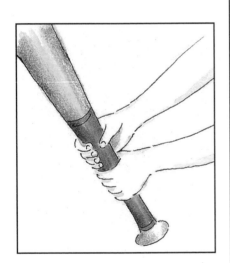

Hold the bat with your fingers instead of the palms of your hands. If the bat feels too heavy, try choking up a little to make it easier to swing.

BATTING BASICS

It's time to step up to the plate. As you practice, try to swing your bat the same way every time. Get into the habit of swinging smoothly without thinking about it.

ON YOUR MARK!

■ Step into the batter's box and face home plate. Your feet should be a little bit apart.

■ Before you get set, hold your bat over home plate. Make sure the end of your bat extends to the far side of the plate. If it does, you should be able to reach any pitch that crosses the plate within the strike zone.

GET SET!

■ Now take your batting stance. Your bat should point back and up, over your arm and shoulder. Keep

Look at the ball

elbows up

bend your knees

your bat up and your elbows away from your body.

■ Turn your front foot just a bit so it points to the pitcher. Turn your head, too. Look over your front shoulder at the pitcher. Bend your knees and lean back just a bit.

■ Take a deep breath and relax. The bat should feel loose and comfortable in your hands. Don't look at the fielders, the base runners, or your mother in the stands. As you face the pitcher, *look at the ball!*

SWING!

■ As the pitcher lets go of the ball, take a small step toward it with your front foot. Push with your back foot. Start your swing before the ball reaches home plate.

■ As you swing, be sure to stretch out your arms. Bring your bat smoothly

and evenly over home plate. You want to hit the ball while it's just a bit in front of you.

■ As the ball touches the bat, snap your wrists. Make sure you finish swinging the bat after you hit the ball. If you "follow through" in this way, you'll hit with more power. Now drop the bat and start running!

watch the ball hit the bat

extend your arms— snap wrists

shift weight from back to front leg

follow through

twist body

"When I'm up at bat, I tell myself to relax and just put the bat on the ball. I figure that if I just hit the ball hard someplace, good things are bound to happen."

BUNTING BASICS

A bunt is used to move runners from one base to the next. You can practice this basic bunting style:

■ As the pitcher starts to throw, turn toward him. Bring your back foot forward so your feet are side by side, pointing to the pitcher.

■ Slide your top hand up the bat. Hold the bat loosely with your fingers in the back so the ball won't hit them. The bat should be chest high and reaching across home plate.

■ Watch the ball! Move the bat into position so the ball will hit it. Let the ball strike the bat.

■ Try to make the ball land about halfway between the pitcher and catcher. You want the fielder to take a lot of time getting to it. Meanwhile, your team-mate can run to the next base. You've hit a sacrifice bunt, and even if you're out, you've done a good job for your team.

Bubble Batting

This game helps you learn to control your bat. It will also teach you one of the most important rules of hitting: Keep your eye on the ball, or in this case, on the bubbles! Try playing on a day that is not too windy.

Have your friend take the bubble wand and blow just a few bubbles. Watch the direction they appear to be going. Stand where most of the bubbles will drift right past you.

Now your friend starts blowing lots of bubbles. As the bubbles float your way, swing the bat and pop as many as you can. You can move around a little bit as you try to burst those bubbles. Swing the bat for about a minute. Then switch places and give your friend a turn.

Bopping a bubble can be as hard as hitting a nasty knuckleball. Remember, a big swing has little chance of hitting a bubble dancing on the air. Instead, tap the bubble gently. The secret is to watch each bubble until you hit it and flick the bat with your wrists.

Beach Ball Baseball

RATING: ◍

PLAYERS:
two teams

YOU NEED:
Bat, beach ball, bases

A baseball is a very small target for players who are hitting for the first time. You can solve this problem by thinking big. A beach ball filled with air is much bigger than a baseball and moves more slowly so it's easier to hit. When you hit it, the beach ball will not go as far as the smaller ball does. This also helps when you want to play baseball in a small space, like a backyard.

If you have enough players, you can play a game with two teams using regular baseball rules. Just make sure that the field is smaller and the distance between bases is shorter. You can also play other baseball games with a beach ball.

BEACH DODGEBALL: *This game starts like regular baseball. When a batter hits a pitched beach ball, however, he must run around all the bases. If the fielders catch the ball on a fly, the runner is out. They can also get him out by throwing the beach ball and hitting him with it before he reaches home plate.*

S-W-I-N-G: *In this game, one player hits pitches and everyone else fields. The batter keeps hitting until another player catches the ball. When that happens, the player who caught it gets the letter "S" and takes his turn hitting. The game continues with players catching and hitting. With each catch, the fielder gets a letter and takes a turn hitting. The first person to spell the word S-W-I-N-G is the winner.*

BALLPARK BASEBALL

STICKY BATS

To get a solid grip on their bat, many major-leaguers use pine tar. A bat handle coated with pine tar is less likely to slip out of their hands. Some players keep a supply of the sticky black stuff right on their bat. Look at the spot on the bat above their hands and you may see it. Other players use a rag to wipe pine tar on their bat while waiting on deck.

You don't need to use pine tar, but you should have a good grip on your bat. Wrap some adhesive tape around the bat handle to help you hold it. Or rub your hands with a little dirt each time you step up to the plate. This dries out your sweaty hands and helps you hold on tight.

GLOVE OR NO GLOVE?

Most big-league batters wear thin leather gloves to help them grip the bat. A swinging bat hits a speeding ball with a lot of force. That can make the bat shake and vibrate. On a cool day, vibrations sting a hitter's hands, so he usually wears gloves for protection.

You probably won't need to wear batting gloves. On the other hand, you may have them, and you may discover they help you hold a bat tightly. In that case, go for it!

DIGGING IN

When a batter first steps up to the plate, he takes a moment to get set. He may start scratching in the dirt with his shoe, like a dog pawing at the ground. That batter is digging a spot for his back foot. If he firmly sets his back foot, he can

push forward off it when he swings. Batters who use their whole body—including their legs—hit with more power.

Even when batting on a cement sidewalk, make sure you plant your back foot firmly before every swing. And wear sneakers with bottoms that grip the ground.

DONUTS ON DECK

While waiting on deck, many big-leaguers put a metal ring on their bat. This "donut" makes the bat feel heavier as they practice swinging. (Some batters also swing a small, heavy lead bat.) When it's time to bat, a hitter taps his bat on the ground and the donut slides off. Now his bat feels lighter and easier to swing.

You don't need a donut to make your bat seem lighter. Try swinging two bats at once on deck. When you drop the extra one, your regular bat will feel much easier to swing.

"*Sometimes when I'm on deck, I'll put a donut on the lead bat. After I swing that bat 9 or 10 times, my own bat feels light as a feather. That adds to my confidence. Maybe the last time up the pitcher threw his fastball right by me. Now that my bat's a little quicker, I might catch up with that pitch and hit it out of the park.*"

Sweet Swing

RATING: ⚾⚾

PLAYERS:
2 or more

YOU NEED:
Bat, batting tee, rope, a tree

Batters with a level swing hit the ball harder and more often. This game takes the hills and valleys out of your batting stroke.

To set up the game, hang a rope over a tree branch. Make sure the end of the rope hangs down to the height of the tallest player's shoulders. Place the batting tee directly under the rope. Set the tee so it comes up to the knees of the shortest player. The space between the rope and the tee is the strike zone.

Now step up to the plate. There is no ball in this game. Each player gets five swings through the strike zone. The bat must pass above the tee and below the rope *without hitting either one*. If three of your swings go through, you're still in the game.

Now raise the tee one inch and lower the rope one inch. Players take their swings through this smaller strike zone. After each round, raise the tee and lower the rope so the strike zones will get smaller and smaller.

When a player cannot get at least three swings through the strike zone, he is out of the game. Keep going until there is only one player left. If no player succeeds three times during the final round, then the player with the highest number of successful swings is the winner.

Sock Ball

Sometimes a bag of sock balls beats a bucket of baseballs. A soft sock ball won't go too far when you hit it, and it won't break any windows. With less to worry about, you can concentrate on your hitting.

Use a piece of chalk to mark a large, round target on a wall. (You can use a fence instead of a wall—in that case, use string or yarn to make a target.) Mark off home plate a few feet in front of the wall. Try starting about 10 feet away, but experiment as you play—

you may need to be closer to the wall.

If you are batting first, take your position at home plate. Your friend kneels off to the side about eight feet away. With a gentle under-hand toss, she flips the first sock ball to you. You swing and try to hit it. One by one, your friend pitches socks and you swing your bat. Don't try to clobber every pitch. A quick, easy swing with lots of wrist action works best.

Score five points for every sock ball that hits the target on the wall. Score three points each time it hits the wall but misses the target. Score one point if you manage to hit the ball but miss the wall.

Now trade places with your friend and pitch to her. The first player to score 21 is the winner. As in base-ball, your friend gets last licks. If both players score over 21, the one with the higher total wins.

BATTING RECORDS

HIT! Mickey Mantle is famous for hitting some of the longest home runs ever. One of his best shots took place in 1953 while he was playing against the Washington Senators. Mickey crushed a baseball that sailed over the fence, over the bleachers and

right out of Griffith Stadium. It was later found 565 feet from home plate!

MISS! Reggie Jackson is one of the greatest clutch players and home run hitters of all time. Like most big swingers, he missed a lot of pitches, too. Reggie holds the career record with 2,597 strikeouts.

HIT! When it comes to heavy hitters, no one can

beat Edd Roush. During their careers Hank Aaron hit 687 more home runs and Pete Rose had 1,880 more base hits, but Roush swung the heaviest bat. It weighed 48 ounces. Roush swung his fat bat well enough to be elected to Baseball's Hall of Fame.

MISS! Most pitchers are not very good hitters. One of the worst performances ever was turned in by pitcher Bob Buhl. In 1962 he was "0" for the season. Buhl came to the plate 70 times and did not get a single base hit.

MISS! Pitcher Hoyt Wilhelm smacked a home

run in his very first at-bat in the big leagues. He

565 feet!

never hit another one in his 21-year career.

HIT! Who is the greatest home run hitter of all time? In the United States it's Hank Aaron, who collected 755 home runs in his career. In the world it's Sadaharu Oh. The Japanese slugger hit 868 home runs!

HIT! Jay Clarke had the greatest hitting day in minor-league history. Clarke got up eight times in a game and hit eight home runs. His team won the game 51 to 3!

Flies Up

RATING: ⚾ ⚾ ⚾

PLAYERS:
2 or more

YOU NEED: Bat, ball (a batting tee is optional)

This batting game combines two great sports—baseball and bowling. It works best in a schoolyard or on some other smooth playing surface. Choose one person to be the first batter. All other players take the field. Since this is a game of fly balls, everyone should set up in the outfield.

Now the batter gets to work. She tosses the ball up and hits it. The batter gets three swings. She must hit a fly ball that lands before anyone can catch it. If she does, she gets three more swings. If a fielder catches a fly ball before it bounces, the batter places the bat on the ground in front of her.

Now the fielder who caught the ball takes aim. From the spot where he caught the ball, he rolls it toward the bat. If the ball hits the bat, the fielder trades places with the batter. He keeps hitting until he fails to hit a fly ball or a bowler knocks him out of the batter's box.

Hitting fly balls is a real challenge, and so is hitting the bat with the ball. If this game is too hard, you can play with simpler rules. Have the batter hit either a fly ball *or* a ground ball. Now the fielders can move closer. The fielders still try to roll the ball at the bat after any clean catch.

Home Run Derby

RATING: ⚾⚾⚾

PLAYERS:
2 or more

YOU NEED:
Bat, ball

This is a game for really big swingers. Mark a line in the outfield using string or chalk, not too far from home plate. Pretend this line is the outfield fence, and any baseball that lands behind it is a home run.

The players who are not batting should gather just in front of the line that repre-sents the outfield fence. They cannot step over that line, but they can reach up and try to catch the ball or knock it down to prevent a home run.

Each batter tosses the ball up and hits it. He gets 10 swings, and each swing should be a big one. There are no singles, doubles or triples. Swing "for the fences." Score one point for each home run you hit.

After every player has taken a turn at bat, the one with the most home runs wins. You can also play this game in teams. First a player from one team swings, and then a player from the other. At the end, the team with the most home runs is the winner.

*" **I** always wanted to excel in all parts of the game, so when I found something I couldn't do, it made me want to work harder. I still do drills every day, and you should, too. That's the only way you can get better."*

NO-FRILLS DRILLS

A major-league baseball game lasts about three hours, but players typically spend eight hours or more at the ballpark. A lot of that time is spent getting ready to play. You can use these batting drills to work on the parts of your game you need to practice.

BATTING TEE DRILL

Purpose: To learn to hit all pitches in your strike zone.

Place a batting tee on home plate. Set the tee so the ball is on the inside corner at the batter's knees. From this tee position, hit five balls as hard as you can. Repeat with the tee in the following positions.

■ Inside corner, chest high

■ Outside corner, knee high

■ Outside corner, chest high

Concentrate on keeping your swing level and hitting hard line drives. (To save time chasing after the balls, set up the plate and tee so you hit the ball into a batting cage.)

BUNTING DRILL

Purpose: To learn bunting technique.

Have the bunter set up at home plate. Four fielders play the parts of pitcher, first baseman, third baseman, and catcher. Each stands about 20 feet from the batter. The pitcher tosses the ball and the batter tries to place a bunt in front of each fielder. After she does, all players, including the hitter, exchange positions and the drill continues. Take turns until everyone has bunted.

PEPPER DRILL

Purpose: To learn to control the bat.

This is one of baseball's most popular drills. Three fielders stand in a line about 20 feet from a batter. The batter tosses the ball up and swings down slightly, hitting a ground ball. The fielder who scoops it up tosses the ball back to the batter. He hits that return toss back at the fielders and the drill continues.

Remember to take a soft half-swing at the ball. Always swing down a bit so you hit ground balls. You may want to add one more player as a catcher. If you swing and miss, the catcher can flip the ball to you so the drill can continue.

BETTER BATTING DRILL

Purpose: To practice hitting with runners on base.

Batting practice is your best opportunity to work on your batting stroke, but it's also the time to work on batting plays you might need in a game. Follow this sequence when you take your practice swings:

■ First two swings—Bunt with each swing.

■ Third swing—*Hit and run.* Try to hit a ground ball so a runner could get to second.

■ Fourth swing—*Move the runner to third.* Hit a ground ball toward first and second base.

■ Fifth swing—*Score the run.* Hit a long fly ball to outfield.

■ The rest of your swings—Work on hitting the ball hard.

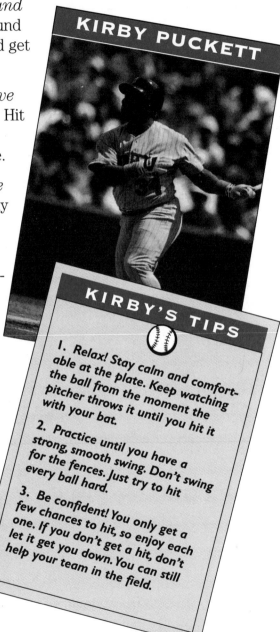

KIRBY PUCKETT

KIRBY'S TIPS

1. Relax! Stay calm and comfortable at the plate. Keep watching the ball from the moment the pitcher throws it until you hit it with your bat.

2. Practice until you have a strong, smooth swing. Don't swing for the fences. Just try to hit every ball hard.

3. Be confident! You only get a few chances to hit, so enjoy each one. If you don't get a hit, don't let it get you down. You can still help your team in the field.

On the Bases

"When I was young, I wasn't the biggest of strongest player—but I was always one of the fastest. Even if you're not one of the fastest, you can still be a good base runner. The trick is to learn to make the most of the speed you have. some of the best base runners aren't fast, but they're smart!"

Bats, balls and gloves are only some of the things you need to play baseball. Luckily, you already have two of the most important pieces of equipment you will ever need—your feet! Baseball is a running game. When you circle the bases, chase after a loose baseball in the field, or steal home, you've got to move fast.

Some people are faster than others. Speed helps, but you need to *think* fast as well as run fast, and make good decisions when you are on the move.

BASEBALL TALK

INSIDE-THE-PARK HOME RUN *A play on which a batter gets around all the bases even though the ball is not hit over the fence.*

LEAD *When a base runner takes a few steps off one base toward the next base before the pitcher throws the ball.*

RUNDOWN *A play on which a runner is trapped between two bases. The fielders must throw the ball back and forth until they can tag him out.*

SLIDE *When a runner drops to the ground and skids—feet or head first—into a base.*

STEAL *A play on which a base runner runs for the next base as a pitcher throws the ball to home plate. She must get there before the catcher throws* the ball to the base and she is tagged out.

STOLEN BASE *A successful steal.*

TAG-UP *A play on which a runner tries to advance on a fly ball out. The runner must wait on the base until the ball is caught and then beat the throw and the tag at the next base.*

FAST FEET

You don't need anybody to teach you how to run. You have been running for most of your life, and going faster as you have grown. Even so, there are a few basic things to remember:

■ When you run, be sure to stay on the balls of your feet—that's the front part near your toes. Always point your toes straight ahead and run in a straight line.

■ Run with your feet *and* your arms. Pump your arms up and down as you run.

■ As you run, take medium-size steps. Your stride should feel smooth, steady and comfortable.

RUNNING BASICS

Practice your running style as you take a trip around the bases.

FIRST BASE

As soon as you hit a ball, the race begins. Can you get to first base before the ball does?

■ Drop your bat and go, go, go! As you start to run, step with your back foot first. That's the quickest way to get going.

■ Run in a straight line. As you near first base, *don't slow down*. Baseball rules allow you to run straight *past* first base. Just be sure to step on the base as you go by it!

SECOND BASE

If you know you will be safe at first, you may want to head for second base. That changes the way you run just a bit.

■ Before you reach first base, start to swing out into foul territory. You should be about two-thirds of the way down the base path when you make your move.

■ As you reach first, step on the *inside corner* of the base with your right foot. That gets your body moving in the right direction to go to second.

■ As you turn past first, make sure you know where the ball is. Run as fast as you can to second base in a straight line.

THIRD BASE

If the ball still is loose or far away, you may be able to head for third.

Your Home run diagram

■ Curve around second base the same way you ran around first. Touch the inside corner with your right foot. Run as fast as you can.

■ As you approach third base, look over at your coach for help.

If he holds his hands up, stop at third. That's as far as you should go.

If he gets on his knees and puts his hand on the ground, look out! Slide if you know how. If not, try to stay away from the fielder in case she tries to tag you.

If he swings one arm in a big circle, keep going. Step on the inside corner of third base and head for home.

HOME PLATE

Don't stop now, you're almost there!

■ Put your head down and *run*. As your coach did at third base, the next batter will signal you if there is going to be a close play at home plate.

■ Don't slow down. Touch home as you run past it. Congratulations, you made it!

SLIDING BASICS

When you arrive at a base at the same time as the ball, you may need to slide. Sliding lets you get low to the ground so you are harder to tag. It's a good idea to have an adult help you learn to slide. Good sliding takes practice, and practice will cut down on your chance of getting hurt.

■ Start your slide before you reach the base. Put one leg forward as you start to fall back on the seat of your pants. Lean back just a bit so your body starts to stretch out.

■ Bend your back leg under your lead leg. As you fall, you should land on the upper part of your bent leg and on your rear end. Keep your arms and hands up and out of the way.

Ball Tag

RATING: ◐

PLAYERS: 3 or more

YOU NEED: Ball, glove

Baseball players often run in short, quick bursts, and tag games also use speed and quickness. Play this one on a field or in a park with lots of room to run. Set some boundaries in the field for the game.

One player is IT. She takes the ball and the glove, and chases after all the others until she catches one player and tags him. When she makes the tag, as in baseball, it *must* be with the ball. (The tag can be made with the ball in her bare hand or in her glove hand.) When she tags someone, she hands him the ball and glove. Now it's his turn to be IT.

There are no bases where players can rest, and runners must stay on the field at all times. Players learn to move fast or be caught.

Base Tag

This game uses bases and runners. There must be two fewer bases than there are players. For instance, if you have seven players, use five bases.

Spread out the bases all over the field. Start the game using the basic rules of tag. In this game, a runner who steps on a base is

RATING: ⚾

PLAYERS:
5 or more

YOU NEED:
Ball, bases

safe and cannot be tagged.

It sounds easy enough, but here is the rule that makes things trickier: There can be only one person on a base. If a new runner steps on base, the runner who is waiting there must leave. Since there is always someone without a base, runners on base have

to think ahead. If they wait until someone touches the base, the player who is doing the tagging may be right next to them. The trick is to get off the base and escape at just the right instant.

Base Race

waits with his foot on base and a baseball cap in his hand.

The race begins when someone shouts "GO!" The first two runners dash around the bases, each with a baseball cap in his hand. They must circle all four bases. As each runner gets back to where he started, the next runner is waiting on the base. She takes the cap from him and runs the bases, then hands the cap to the next player. The first team to finish is the winner.

Teams start at home plate and second base so they will not bump into each other. But sometimes one team is so fast that it catches up to the other one. If a player from one team catches up and tags her opponent, the race is over and her team wins.

This relay race lets you practice the correct style for rounding each base. You need a baseball infield for this race. If you can't use a baseball infield, simply make your own. Place four folded

RATING: ⚾
PLAYERS: 6 or 8
YOU NEED: Bases, 2 caps

towels on the grass or use chalk to make bases on a playground.

Divide the players into two teams. One team stands at second base and the other at home plate. The first runner for each team

Change Bases

Runners often must decide quickly which base to run to. This game helps keep you on your toes. It's a good game for a playground or schoolyard.

To begin, have all the players form a circle around one person. There should be about 10 steps between

RATING: ⚾

PLAYERS: 4 or more

YOU NEED: Chalk

players in the circle. Draw a base with chalk where each person in the circle is standing.

Each player standing on the base is ready to go. Suddenly the player in the middle takes off for a base. When they see him on the go, all other players must also run to a

new base. Since there is one more person than there are bases, someone will be left without a base. He gets a point and stands in the middle to start the next round. Play until one person has collected five points. At that time, the player or players with the *lowest* scores are the winners.

BALLPARK BASEBALL

FIRST THINGS FIRST

When a runner gets to first base, the coach reminds him how many outs there are. That helps the runner know what to do if the next batter hits the ball. Major-league players follow some basic running rules.

eyes on the ball! →

bend your knees and get ready to run.

step off with your lead foot.

If no one is out, play it safe. Go to second on a base hit to the outfield, but then be careful. Don't make the first out of an inning while trying to get to third.

If there is one out, go for it! Try getting to third on an outfield hit. If you do, you may be able to score a run if the next batter hits a ground ball or a fly ball out.

If there are two outs, go one base at a time. You may be able to score from second base on a hit to the outfield. Never make the third out at third base.

STEP BY STEP

When a runner is on base, he should usually take a lead. By moving a few steps toward the next base he shortens the distance he must run. That makes it easier to steal the base or to get there quickly when the batter hits the ball. (Runners also take a few quick steps as the pitcher lets go of the ball.)

Be careful when you take a lead. Be sure the pitcher has the ball when you step off the base. And make sure you can get back to the base safely if she throws the ball to the fielder waiting there.

be sure you can reach the base if you have to run back.

RUNNING FOUL

A major-league infield has white chalk lines running from home plate past first base and third base. You might think players would run on this line, but they don't. Instead, they run a bit outside the line, in foul territory. If a runner is hit by a ball in fair territory, he's out. To play it safe, runners stay in foul territory whenever possible.

You should also stay in foul territory when running from home plate to first base. If you are on third base, be sure to step off the base on the foul side of the line.

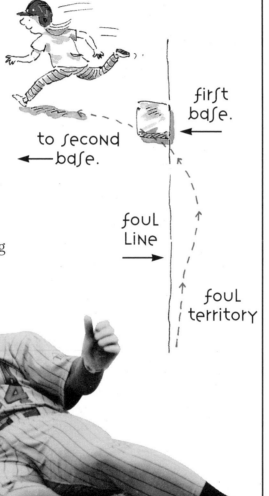

first base.

to second base.

foul line →

foul territory

HEADS OR HEELS?

On a close play a runner will often slide into the base to beat the throw. While some players use the basic feet-first slide, others prefer going into the base head first. A head-first slide allows a runner to slip his hand past a fielder's glove. Unfortunately, his head and hand are more likely to get stepped on or hit by the ball.

When you are first starting out, stick to feet-first slides. And when you do slide, remember to get up quickly. If the ball gets past the fielder, you will be ready to take an extra base.

*" **I** always slide feet first, because I never learned to slide any other way. Some base stealers like Rickey Henderson go in head first, but I never do. If I tried that, I'd probably break something!"*

Home Run Race

RATING: ◍ ◍

PLAYERS:
two full teams

YOU NEED:
Ball, bat, gloves, bases

An inside-the-park home run is one of the most exciting plays in baseball. In this game every single at-bat is either a home run or an out. Choose up sides and take the field, as you would in a regular baseball game.

The first batter steps up to the plate. She swings and hits the ball. She runs to first base and then keeps right on going around the bases. To get her out, the fielders must throw the ball to first, second, third and home. If the ball makes it to home plate before the runner does, she is out. If not, she scores a run for her team. Each team gets three outs per inning. Play a five-inning game.

Running Bases

Baseball runners often must make important decisions in an instant. In Running Bases you need to move and think fast, too.

Set up two bases. They should be extra-large since there must be room for lots of runners. Your bases should be closer together than those on a baseball field. Experiment to find the distance that works best for you and your friends.

RATING: 🌑🌑

PLAYERS:
6 or more

YOU NEED: Ball, 2 gloves, 2 large bases or chalk

Now have a fielder stand on each base. The rest of the players crowd onto the bases. As the game begins the fielders toss the ball to each other.

Suddenly a runner dashes for the other base. One of the fielders must tag the runner with the ball before she gets there. If he does, that runner is out of the game. The other runners continue, going back and forth between the two bases.

Runners can try different strategies. Some runners wait until a ball is dropped before ever trying to steal a base. Others take off and then suddenly stop between the bases on purpose. Tossing the ball back and forth, the fielders close in and try to tag the runner. If she's quick, she may sneak past them and escape to a base. Sometimes runners use teamwork. If everyone dashes at once, some people are sure to make it!

The game continues until all the runners except two have been tagged out. Those runners get to be the fielders for the next round.

Raceball

RATING: 🔵🔵

PLAYERS:
4 or more

YOU NEED:
Rubber ball,
tennis ball

Runners are not the only baseball players on the go. Fielders must move fast to get to the ball. Try this game on a field or some other wide open space. Be sure to use a *soft* rubber ball or a tennis ball.

While one player holds a ball, the others spread out in the field. They form a line about 10 feet in front of the player with the ball. Their backs are turned so they cannot see her or what she is about to do. Without warning, she fires a ball over their heads and past them.

The race begins the moment the players in the field see the ball go by them. Each one runs and tries to be the one to pick up the ball. Whoever does it scores one point and gets to make the next throw.

Now the players spread out from the spot where the ball was picked up. Once again they turn their backs to the person with the ball, he makes a throw, and the game continues. The first player to pick up five points is the winner.

RUNNING RECORDS

SAFE! While playing for the Chicago White Sox, Herman Schaefer became the only man in history to steal first base. Schaefer was standing on second when he suddenly took off for first. He wanted to confuse the catcher so his teammate could score from third. He slid into first with a backwards stolen base!

SAFE! On May 6, 1975, Bob Watson made baseball history. The Houston Astros' first baseman scored major-league baseball's *one millionth* run.

OUT! Rickey Henderson set the record for stolen bases in a season when he swiped 130 in 1982. But the Oakland A's left fielder also set a record that year for being thrown out while stealing 42 times.

SAFE! When Jimmy Piersall hit the 100th home run of his career he had a special way of celebrating. The New York Mets outfielder ran around the bases—backwards!

SAFE! Vince Coleman once stole 50 bases in a row without being caught. While playing for the St. Louis Cardinals, Coleman began the streak in the 1988 season and finished it in 1989.

OUT! Babe Herman was the key to one of baseball's most famous base-running goofs. While batting with the bases loaded, Babe Herman hit a ball off the outfield wall.

Running as hard as he could, he steamed into third base only to find two of his Brooklyn Dodger teammates standing there. The third baseman tagged Babe and the runner in front of him. Babe wanted to knock in three runs with a triple. Instead, he doubled into a double play.

SAFE! Herb Washington was a track star who was given a baseball job by the Oakland A's. During the 1974 and 1975 seasons, the team used the speedster as a pinch runner. Washington played in 105 games without taking a single at-bat. Even so, he stole 31 bases and scored 33 runs.

Base Burglar

This game for three players challenges you to be a big-time base stealer. The setup is just like Running Bases, except this time there is only one runner. The other two players are the fielders on the bases. While the runner starts on one base, the fielder at the other one has the ball.

As the game begins, the fielder with the ball throws it to the other fielder. At that instant the runner takes off. When the other fielder catches the ball he throws it back as quickly as possible so the first fielder can tag the runner.

If a runner is quick enough, he will beat the throw and steal the base. If not, he must stop between the bases. The fielders close in, tossing the ball back and forth. If they tag the runner, he is out. If he escapes the rundown and scrambles into either base, he gets credit for a steal.

A player remains the runner as long as he steals bases. When he's finally tagged out, he takes the place of one of the fielders. Play until everyone has had a turn as a runner.

Capture the Glove

RATING: ◊◊◊

PLAYERS:
8 or more

YOU NEED:
A glove or cap for each player

This is a great game for two teams with lots of players. Make sure each person has a glove. If you don't have enough gloves to go around, use baseball caps or anything else that is handy.

Mark a line down the center of a large field to split it into two equal parts. Each team will defend one side.

The players put their gloves in a row to mark the back line of their team's territory.

Now the game begins. Each team tries to steal all the gloves from the other side of the field. To do this, they must cross into enemy territory and get to a glove without being tagged. If a player reaches a glove, he

is safe. He can carry it out and add the glove to his team's back line. If a player is tagged before he gets to a glove, he is captured. He must stand out of bounds behind that team's row of gloves.

Teammates plot and work together. Sometimes one player will make a dash. With everyone chasing her, another player can sneak in and grab a glove. The game ends when one team has all the gloves or when they have captured all the players from the other team.

You can add another twist to this game. A player who reaches the glove can carry it out, or she can tag a captured teammate. That player is then free to go back with her and return to the game.

NO-FRILLS DRILLS

SLIDING DRILL

Purpose: To develop sliding technique.

In this drill there should be a base for every player. The bases are lined up and the players stand the length of a base path away. Each player dashes for her base and slides.

Work on your technique. Remember to kick out your front leg and tuck your back one underneath. Be sure to notice where your slide ends. Did you come up short or slide right past the base? Learn to pick the right spot in front of the base to start your slide.

Be sure to pick a soft, grassy place to practice your sliding. If you can, wet the grass a bit with a garden hose before you start. That makes sliding easier to practice. Remember to get an adult to help if you're learning to slide for the first time.

TAG-UP DRILL

Purpose: To practice scoring on a fly-ball out.

Three players are needed for this drill—a base runner, a catcher and an outfielder. The base runner leads off third base as the catcher throws a fly ball to the outfielder. The runner then returns to third and waits with his foot on the base, but the instant the ball is caught, he dashes for home. The outfielder throws the ball, and the catcher tries to make the tag before the runner crosses the plate.

In this drill each player works on different skills. The runner learns to blast off from third base the exact instant the ball is caught, and slide past the catcher on a close play. The outfielder practices getting in position and making strong, accurate throws. The catcher develops his skill blocking the path of the runner and hanging on to the ball as he makes a tag.

BASE-RUNNING DRILL

Purpose: To work on the mental side of base running.

While your teammates take batting practice, you can practice your base running.

■ Start at first base. As the pitcher throws the ball to the hitter, work on getting a good jump off first base. Take several quick steps toward second each time the pitcher starts to let go of the ball.

■ Move down to second. Take your lead and work on "reading" the way the ball comes off the bat. How quickly can you tell if it is a fly ball or a grounder? Decide whether to break for third or play it safe and return to second.

■ Now go to third. Work on tagging up on fly balls. Also, work on breaking for home the instant the batter hits a ground ball.

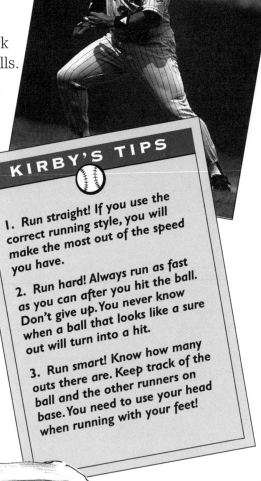

KIRBY PUCKETT

KIRBY'S TIPS

1. **Run straight!** If you use the correct running style, you will make the most out of the speed you have.

2. **Run hard!** Always run as fast as you can after you hit the ball. Don't give up. You never know when a ball that looks like a sure out will turn into a hit.

3. **Run smart!** Know how many outs there are. Keep track of the ball and the other runners on base. You need to use your head when running with your feet!

Playing the Field

*" **I** use a glove for about three years before it falls apart. I always have another one ready to go. It takes two or three weeks to break in a new glove. To soften it up, I play a lot of catch with it. I take a bat and pound it into the pocket. I beat it up as much as I can. Sometimes I even roll my truck tire over it!"*

Sooner or later, baseball becomes a game of catch. Whether the ball is bouncing, rolling, floating, dipping or soaring, you have to be ready to grab it.

GRAB YOUR GLOVE

Baseball bats and balls are basically the same. But a baseball glove—*your* baseball glove—is a special piece of equipment. You need to choose the right one and take good care of it.

Baseball gloves come in several different designs. Catchers use round mitts with lots of padding to take the sting out of fast pitches. First basemen have large gloves shaped for scooping up throws. Most infielders use slightly smaller gloves so they can pull the ball out for quick throws. Outfielders like bigger gloves with deep pockets.

You should start out with a basic glove that feels comfortable but is big enough for your growing hand. If you're a righty, slip your left hand inside it. Make a fist with your right hand and pound it into the middle or "pocket." If you're a lefty, put the glove on your right hand.

GLOVE LOVE

A new leather glove is stiff. As you play baseball with it, the glove will get softer and easier to use. You can help it along.

■ Bend the glove back and forth. This will soften it up and make it more flexible.

■ Buy special oil for a glove. Rubbing it with this oil will make the leather softer.

■ Put a baseball in your glove when you're not using it. Use rubber bands to hold the glove closed around it. After a while, the glove pocket will take the shape of the ball.

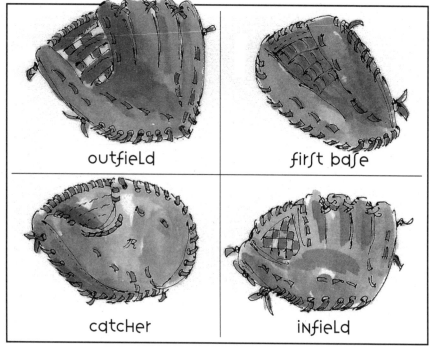

outfield

first base

catcher

infield

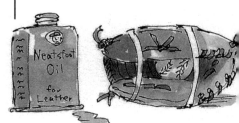

BASEBALL TALK

FIELDER'S CHOICE
A play on which fielders choose to tag out a base runner instead of tagging the player who hit the ball.

FORCE-OUT *When a fielder with the ball touches a base before the runner gets there, the runner is out. This only happens when the runner cannot go back to the base from which he came.*

DOUBLE PLAY
A play in which fielders | *record two outs on one batted ball.*

TRIPLE PLAY
A play in which fielders get three players out on one batted ball.

PASSED BALL
A pitched ball that gets past a catcher, allowing a base runner to move to the next base.

TAG *To touch the runner with the ball in your hand or glove. If the runner is not on a base, he is out.*

FIELDING BASICS

You never know when a ball will come your way, so be ready on every pitch.

GET READY

■ Stand with your legs apart. Bend your knees just a little and lean forward. Your weight should be on your toes.

■ Rest your glove and your hand lightly on your knees.

■ Use the time between pitches to relax, but focus on each pitch. When someone hits the ball your way, get going!

GET SET

■ If a ball is hit in your direction, move quickly toward it. Run to a spot where the ball will come right to you. This is known as "getting in front of the ball." Never take your eyes off the ball as you run to meet it.

■ Pound your glove with your fist as you run. This will make sure your glove is snug on your hand and the pocket is ready to receive the ball.

CATCH A FLY!

■ As you settle under the ball, pound your glove with your fist. Hold the glove with the fingers pointing up. Keep your other hand nearby, too. Your thumbs should almost be touching.

■ Try to catch the ball while holding your glove a bit in front of your body. In that position it is easiest to move your glove up or down if you need to. As you catch the ball, use your other hand to cover the ball and glove. Then grab the ball and throw it.

GRAB A GROUND BALL!

■ Bend your knees and put your glove near the ground. The fingers of the glove should point down, facing out. Keep your other hand just above the glove and keep your eyes on that bouncing ball!

■ Move your glove so the ball bounces into it. When it does, quickly cover your glove with your other hand. Are you sure you have the ball? Then take it out of your glove and make your throw.

■ Sometimes you will not have time to get in front of the ball. When that happens, bend your knees and reach with your glove. Watch the ball go into it and snap your glove

LOW FLIES AND HIGH BOUNCES: *If a fly ball is sinking in front of you, point your glove fingers down, in grounder position, to make a catch. If a ground ball bounces high, point your glove hand up and catch it like a fly ball.*

shut. Be sure to straighten up before you try to throw the ball.

"**W**hen I was young I was fast, so sometimes I would just outrun the ball. Not any more! Now I have to plan ahead. I may not be as fast as I once was, but I still take a lot of pride in my defense. I work at it every day. I come to the park early and take a lot of fly balls when I practice. I like to see the different angles the ball comes at me. Then in a game, any situation I see is one that I've practiced, so I know I'll be ready."

Hot Potato

RATING: ⚾

PLAYERS:
4 or more

YOU NEED:
A rubber ball or tennis ball

Fielders can't afford to hold the ball too long, and neither can you when you play this game. All the players except one form a circle. That extra person is in charge of the first round of the game. As the game begins, players flip the ball across the circle to each other. There is no special order to the throws. A player can toss it to anyone she wants.

The extra player stands with her back to the circle. When she shouts "Freeze," the throwing stops. If a player is caught holding the ball, she steps out of the circle. If the ball is in the air, then the player who is about to catch it steps out.

The game continues in the same way. One by one the players leave the circle. The final player left is the winner. She gets to be in charge of the next game.

Bottle Catch

RATING: ◐

PLAYERS: 2

YOU NEED:
A rubber ball,
2 plastic half-
gallon milk jugs

A fast-moving ball may hit your glove and bounce right out of it. This game develops the "soft hands" that will help you hold onto the ball. Before you start, carefully cut off the bottom half of the milk jug. Ask an adult for help. Now turn the jug top upside down and hold it in one hand.

Toss the ball up in the air. Try to catch it in your bottle catcher. Toss it higher each time. As the ball hits the bottle, bring your hand down gently. If you move the bottle catcher in the same direction that the ball is going, the ball is less likely to bounce out of it. (In baseball, as you catch the ball, move your glove so you bring the ball toward your body.) See if you can toss and catch five in a row.

Cut the bottom of another bottle and have a catch with a friend. Score one point for each catch you make. Play until someone collects 11 points.

Bouncers

RATING: 🟢
PLAYERS: 2
YOU NEED:
A ball, 2 gloves

To start this game, players stand about 10 feet apart, or a bit less if you think you need to be closer. Throw a ball so it bounces once before it reaches your friend. He grabs it in his glove and returns a one-bounce throw for you to catch.

Now throw the ball on two bounces back and forth. Keep adding a bounce with each throw. You may need to step farther apart as the bounces add up. How many bounces can you throw without a miss? Now try again and see if you and your friend can keep the game going for even more bounces.

BALLPARK BASEBALL

LEFT IS ALL RIGHT

While your favorite team is warming up on the field, take a lefty count. How many players are wearing baseball gloves on their right hand? Those left-handed players are almost always outfielders, first basemen or pitchers. Playing other positions is much harder for lefties. When they catch a ball, they often must turn all the way around to make a throw to first base. Try throwing lefty from some of the other positions and you'll get the idea.

If you are left-handed, you may find that it's hard playing certain positions, too. But don't be discouraged. There is plenty of room on a baseball team for lefties. Babe Ruth and Lou Gehrig were left-handed. So are Barry Bonds and Ken Griffey Jr!

BACK FINGER

Most major-league fielders do not put all their fingers inside their glove. They slip on their glove so one finger is outside in the back. A hard baseball hits a soft leather glove with a lot of force. Keeping one finger outside takes some of the sting out of catching a fast-moving ball.

back finger

OUTSTANDING IN THE FIELD

Some players always seem to be in the perfect spot when a ball is hit. To find out why, pick a fielder and watch him get set for every hitter in an inning. You will notice that he moves to a slightly different spot for each batter. Sometimes he even moves between pitches to the same batter. A fielder has a lot to think about *before* the ball is hit. Does the batter have the power to reach the fences? Does he usually hit the ball to left, right, or up the middle? The number of outs and runners on base also changes the position where a fielder stands. For example, the shortstop and second baseman take a step toward second base when there is a runner on first, in case there is a play there.

When you play the field, think ahead. Should you cover a particular base? Does the batter hit the ball far? Is she an extra-fast runner? Where did she hit the ball last time? Use this information to get set before each pitch.

IT TAKES TEAMWORK

When you watch a game, your eyes naturally follow the ball to the fielder catching it. Next time, try watching one of his teammates instead. On some plays every fielder seems to be in motion. Catchers follow the batter to first base. Pitchers

often back up the third baseman or catcher. Outfielders move behind their teammate making the catch.

When you play, back up your teammates. Don't relax when you see that the ball isn't coming to you. Think about what's happening and go to a spot where you can help—just in case.

" *I've played every position except shortstop and first base. I play right field now, but I played center field for most of my career. The center fielder is the boss in the outfield. He calls the shots. Catchers and shortstops also get to take charge. So if you're the kind of person who likes to run things, try playing one of these positions."*

Errors

RATING: ⚾ ⚾
PLAYERS: 2
YOU NEED:
Ball, 2 gloves

The goal is to make the other player drop the ball. Throw a ball back and forth with another player. Try different kinds of throws, including ground balls, line drives and pop-ups. Add tricky spins to your throws. Toss the ball so your opponent must turn to one side or the other. You can make any type of throw except a totally wild one.

When a player drops the ball, that counts as an error. If he makes a bad throw, that also counts as an error against him. The first player to make seven errors loses.

Freeze Fly

rest of the team unfreezes.

Score one point for every fly ball your team catches. Subtract one point every time someone makes an error (including any relay throws that your team drops). The first team to score 21 points is the winner.

RATING: 🥎🥎

PLAYERS:
6 or more

YOU NEED:
Ball, gloves

This is a game for two teams of outfielders. Before you start, mark a line down the middle of a field. The two teams now spread out on opposite sides. Players must stay at least 10 feet behind the line.

One player tosses a high fly ball over the line. The other team must catch the ball before it bounces. Any player on the team can catch it. As soon as he does, all players on his team must freeze. Now he throws a fly ball to the other team, or he can make a relay throw to one of his teammates who is closer to the line. She then unfreezes and throws the fly ball for him. Then the

FIELDING RECORDS

CATCH! In the 1880s, most big-leaguers did not use gloves. Second base-man Fred "Sure Shot" Dunlap played second base barehanded and *four times* led the league in fielding.

CATCH! A triple play is a rare event in baseball. Imagine making one all by yourself *and* doing it in the World Series. In 1920, Bill Wambsganss was playing second base for the Cleveland Indians against the Brooklyn Dodgers. There were no outs and two men on base when the batter hit a sharp line drive headed for the outfield. Wambsganss caught the ball on a fly. He stepped on sec-ond base before the runner there could get back to it, and then tagged the other runner who was still coming from first. That's one, two, three outs—an unassisted triple play!

ERROR! While playing outfield for the Texas Rangers, Jose Canseco raced to the fence to catch a fly ball. Unfortunately, he misjudged the ball. Instead of landing in his glove, the ball bounced off his head and over the fence for a home run. Jose was more embarrassed than hurt.

CATCH! Left-handed catchers in the big leagues are unheard of—almost. In 1958, the Chicago Cubs needed to find a backup catcher. Lefty first baseman Dale Long stepped in and caught two games for the Chicago Cubs that year.

CATCH! There are nine positions on the field and nine innings, so it's possible to play an inning at every single position during a game. Bert Campenaris of the Oakland A's played everywhere during one game in 1965. Three years later Cesar Tovar did it while playing for the Minnesota Twins.

CATCH! Gabby Street caught one of the highest flies in history. A fellow player tossed a ball from the top of the Washington Monument. It fell 555 feet to Gabby. It took three tries, but Gabby finally grabbed it!

C-L-U-T-C-H

RATING: ⚾⚾⚾

PLAYERS:
2 or more

YOU NEED:
Rubber ball, wall

This game is part catch and part follow-the-leader. The first player throws the ball off the wall and catches it. She can try a simple throw and catch, but it's more fun to go for a fancy one. For instance, she might throw the ball off the wall and catch it in her cap. Or she could grab it while standing on one foot. Or throw it, spin all the way around, and catch the ball as it comes bouncing back.

If the leader makes her catch, the next player must make the exact same throw and catch. If he catches it, then the next person must do it, too. Keep going until a player misses the ball. That player gets a C—the first letter in CLUTCH.

The next player in turn now tries a different crazy throw and catch. Keep going round and round. Anytime a player makes a catch, the others must follow the lead until someone misses. Every time a player misses, he gets a letter. When a player spells C-L-U-T-C-H, he's out of the game. The last player left is the winner.

Charge It

RATING: ⚾ ⚾ ⚾
PLAYERS: 2
YOU NEED:
Ball, gloves

Outfielders need to come in quickly to grab ground balls. Play this game with a friend to practice charging the ball.

While you start in center field, your friend stands on the pitcher's mound. Your friend throws a ground ball to the outfield. Run in as far as you can and scoop up

that ground ball. Get down on one knee as you catch it so the ball stays in front of you. Throw the ball back to the pitcher's mound and get set at the spot where you caught the ball.

As your friend throws again, you charge another grounder. Each time you catch the ball, you get closer

to the infield. It's okay to drop the ball, but don't let it get past you. If you do, you must go back and continue from the spot where you pick up the ball.

See how many catches it takes for you to reach the edge of the infield diamond. Score one point for each catch. Now switch places with your friend and give him a chance. The player with the lowest score wins.

POP-UP DRILL

Purpose: To learn teamwork between players on fly balls.

One player sets up between first and second. Another player sets up behind her in right field. Now a third player throws short fly balls between them. Both players go for the ball. If the outfielder can reach the ball, she shouts "Mine!" or "I got it!" and the infielder gets out of the way. If not, he keeps going and tries to catch it. Work together so the ball is caught every time without any crashes.

NO-FRILLS DRILLS

NO-LOOK TOSS

Purpose: To judge the location of a fly ball.

This drill helps develop two skills. A player learns to see the flight of a ball in the air and to judge where it will land. One player stands in the outfield with her back to a teammate who has a ball. As he throws a high fly, he shouts "BALL!" The other player must turn, figure out where the ball is going and catch it. Start by throwing fly balls to either side of the fielder. As she gets the hang of it, try throwing fly balls in front of her and behind her.

DIAMOND DRILL

Purpose: To practice catching ground balls and taking throws.

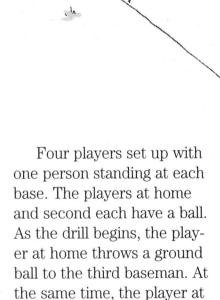

Four players set up with one person standing at each base. The players at home and second each have a ball. As the drill begins, the player at home throws a ground ball to the third baseman. At the same time, the player at second throws a grounder to first.

The third baseman must catch the ball and then turn and throw it to second. The player at first catches the other ball and throws it home. As the two balls are caught, the drill is repeated. The balls move from player to player around the infield. After 10 grounders, switch and have the players at first and third do the throwing.

SIDE-GLIDE DRILL

Purpose: To get in front of the ball when catching it.

One player with a glove stands ready to field. A second player faces him about 10 feet away with a ball in each hand. She rolls a ball to one side of the fielder. He gets in front of the ball, scoops it up and tosses it back to her. As he makes that return throw, his friend rolls the other ball. Now he gets in front of that one and picks it up. Every time he returns one ball, the other one starts rolling his way.

This drill is a great way to work on your footwork, but catching ball after ball without stopping is very tiring. Be sure to take breaks and switch places often.

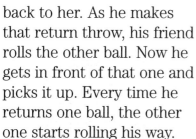

KIRBY PUCKETT

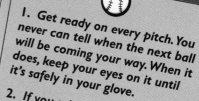

KIRBY'S TIPS

1. Get ready on every pitch. You never can tell when the next ball will be coming your way. When it does, keep your eyes on it until it's safely in your glove.

2. If you miss a ball or drop it, don't stop to feel bad about it. Remember, that ball is still in play, so pick it up and throw it as fast as you can!

3. Try to get every ball that you possibly can. You should feel as if every ball is yours to catch. Don't stop going for that ball unless your teammate lets you know he's got it.

Flips and Fastballs

When you're a fielder, catching a ball is only half your job. As soon as the ball settles in your glove, you must take it out and throw it. Exactly how you do that depends upon where you are on the field. Outfielders throw baseballs the farthest. Infielders toss them straight and fast. Pitchers snap off the trickiest throws of all.

A BALL IN THE HAND

Pick up your baseball and roll it around in your hand. Flip the ball a few inches in the air and catch it. A baseball feels just right for throwing. It weighs about five ounces—not too heavy, but solid enough to go straight on the windiest day. Every baseball is held together by exactly 108 stitches of thread. They help your fingers grip the ball when you're ready to make a throw.

Just as you do with a bat, you must hold a baseball the right way. For basic throwing, your first two fingers go on top of the ball and your thumb underneath it. Are your hands too small for this grip? If they are, try putting three fingers on top. That

BASEBALL TALK

CHANGE-UP *On this pitch, the pitcher's regular arm motion makes the batter expect a fastball. The change in speed causes the batter to swing too soon.*

CURVEBALL *A pitch that bends on its way to home plate.*

ERA *Stands for Earned Run Average. That is the average number of runs a pitcher gives up during nine innings of pitching. A good pitcher has a low ERA.*

KNUCKLEBALL *A pitched ball that flutters and dips in the air as it crosses home plate.*

PITCHER'S MOUND *The raised pile of dirt where a pitcher stands. In the major leagues it is 60' 6" from home plate.*

RELAY *A play on which an outfielder throws the ball to an infielder, who turns and throws to a base.*

SCREWBALL *A pitch that looks to a batter like a spinning curveball, but the ball goes in the opposite direction.*

SINKERBALL *This is a fastball with a difference. The ball moves down as it reaches home plate.*

SLIDER *A pitch thrown like a curveball but faster. It doesn't bend as much, but it happens so fast that the batter has trouble changing his swing to hit it.*

SPLIT-FINGERED FASTBALL *A pitch on which the ball drops as it reaches the batter. When a splitter is thrown slowly it is called a forkball.*

WILD PITCH *A pitch that the catcher cannot reach, allowing a runner to move to the next base.*

extra finger will help, until your hands get bigger.

Be sure those fingers on top touch the stitches on the ball. Always hold a ball with your fingertips and never squeeze too tight.

The basic two-finger grip is shown on the ball that comes with this book. You can use it to make most throws.

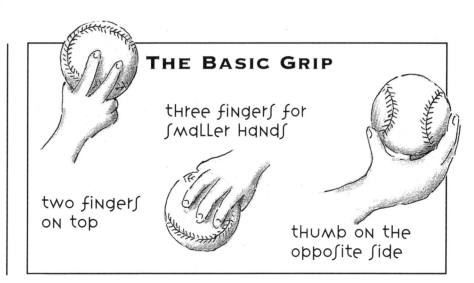

THE BASIC GRIP

three fingers for smaller hands

two fingers on top

thumb on the opposite side

THROWING BASICS

ON YOUR MARK!

■ Grab the ball using the two-finger grip and reach back with your arm.

■ You throw a ball with your arm *and* your legs, so get your feet in the right position. If you're a righty, step forward with your left foot. A lefty steps forward with his right foot.

■ Always step toward the player who will catch your throw. That will point you and the ball in the right direction.

GET SET!

■ Now bring your arm up, so the hand holding the ball is behind your head. If you weren't holding the ball, you would almost be able to scratch behind your ear. Make sure your elbow is away from your body.

■ Lean back just a bit. You should feel most of your weight on your back foot. Now push off that foot and start to step forward.

THROW!

■ As you step, bring your arm forward. The ball should come almost directly over your shoulder.

Look at the player or at his glove

keep your elbow away from your body

step toward the player catching the ball

■ As your arm stretches forward, let go of the ball, making sure to bend your wrist as you throw. That way, the ball will fly faster and straighter.

■ As you let go of the ball, step all the way onto your front foot. Let your arm swing forward with a smooth motion to complete your throw.

*"**N**ever aim the ball when you throw it. When you try to aim it, the ball never seems to go where you want it. Instead, look at the player you're throwing to or look at his glove. That's the best way to put the ball where you want."*

BEGINNER BALL

*I*f you're having trouble throwing the ball for the first time, or if you're helping a younger sibling, try these exercises.

THE ROBIN HOOD: *Pretend you are holding a bow and arrow. Hold the bow in front of you and pull back your arm as if to shoot the arrow. Now you have both arms in position for making a throw.*

THE WHISPERING BALL: *Psssst! The baseball has a secret it wants to tell you. Hold it up just behind your ear so the ball can whisper in it. Throw back your elbow. You are now holding the ball in the right position to make a throw.*

THE HIGH FIVE: *Reach up and give your friend a "high five." Did you notice the way your arm moves forward as you slapped his hand? That's the same basic way your arm moves when you throw a ball.*

Sherwood

MORE THROWS

Here are other throws that might come in handy.

■ Three-quarters:

Throw the ball the same way but not directly over your shoulder. Your arm is still higher than your shoulder, but it is away from your body when you throw.

■ Sidearm:

Now your arm is completely out to the side. If a base runner is in your way, you can use this throw to toss the ball without hitting him.

■ Underhand: Hold

the ball in your fingers with your palm pointing up and flip it. This is for tossing the ball to someone very close to you.

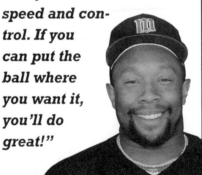

"**D**on't worry about pitches like curveballs or screwballs. Save that fancy stuff for the big leagues. Those pitches are hard to throw and can hurt your arm. Work on speed and control. If you can put the ball where you want it, you'll do great!"

If you can throw a ball fast and straight, you may want to take a turn as pitcher. You can use your basic overhand throw with some slight changes.

GET READY

■ Stand facing the batter. Your glove is in front of you, about waist high.

■ Hold the ball in your throwing hand inside the pocket of your glove.

HERE'S THE WINDUP. . .

■ Raise both arms above your head. Your throwing hand and the ball are still inside your glove. Put your weight on your pitching foot. (If you are right-handed, that's your right foot.)

■ Turn on your pitching foot so that your left shoulder points at the catcher. At the same time, slowly bring your front knee up and your hands down. Your knee and glove will almost touch at your waist. Your weight is on your back foot.

AND THE PITCH!

■ Reach back with your throwing arm, extending your glove hand forward for balance. Step toward the plate with your front foot.

■ As your front foot hits the ground, step and throw. Push hard off your back foot. Finish this step and let your arm keep moving forward after you let go of the ball.

turn on your pitching foot →

knee up, hands down →

↑ show the center fielder the ball

GREAT GRIPS

The basic throw you learned is also called a fastball. Once you've mastered it you can try out fancier pitches. Some, like the curveball and the slider, should be saved until you're older and your arm is stronger—about age 14.

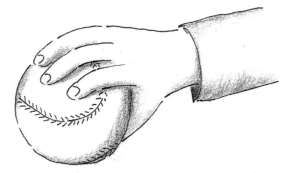

CHANGE-UP: *Hold the ball in the palm of your hand with three fingers on top. As you throw the ball, don't touch it with your fingertips and keep your wrist straight.*

SINKER: *Hold the ball with the fingers on the seams. Throw it like a fastball, making sure your hand stays on top of the ball.*

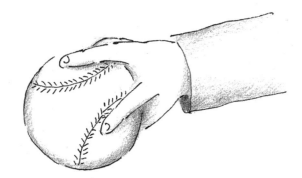

SPLITTER: *The middle and index fingers are just outside the seams. The ball is thrown just like a fastball, with the wrist relaxed. You need really big hands to throw this pitch.*

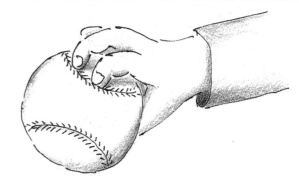

KNUCKLEBALL: *Hold the ball so you can feel your fingernails pressing on it. Push the ball out of your hand. This pitch is so hard to throw that only a few big-leaguers can control it.*

Flipper

RATING: ⚾

PLAYERS:
2 or more in pairs

YOU NEED:
Ball, gloves

In this game two players work as a team. Stand about 10 feet apart and start throwing the ball back and forth. Try to flip it as fast as you can. Any time you drop the ball, pick it up and keep throwing.

Score one point for each throw. How many points can you collect in one minute?

You can also try flipping against other teams. Players set up in pairs. Instead of throwing for a minute, make it a race. Count out loud as you make each throw, and be sure to toss the ball as fast as possible. The first team to make 20 successful throws is the winner.

Strikeout

RATING: ①

PLAYERS:
1 or 2

YOU NEED:
Rubber ball,
wall, chalk

Strikeout is a
pitching game
you can play by your-
self. Draw a strike zone on a
wall. The bottom of this box
should be at your knees.
The top should be at your
shoulders. Make the box
about 15 inches wide.

Pick a spot for your
"pitcher's mound." Now
step up and start pitching.

Every throw that
lands in the box is
a strike. Every one that
lands outside the box is a
ball. Three strikes and the
batter is out. Four balls and
he walks. In baseball, four
walks in an inning might
score a run. Can you strike
out three batters *before* a
run scores?

When you begin to play,

you may throw the ball all
over the place. If that happens, move closer to the
wall. It doesn't matter if
you're only a few feet away
from the wall. The most
important thing is to throw
strikes.

As you get better at
Strikeout, try adding a batter to the game. She stands
next to the strike zone and
swings at your pitches.
(Don't stand too close when
you pitch!) The two of you
can set up rules for hits.
For instance, a ball that
goes past the pitcher is a
single. If it goes past the
mailbox on a fly, that's a
double. Past the telephone
pole is a triple and beyond
the fence is—what else?—a
home run.

Baseball Golf

Throw the ball until you hit it. Go from one hole to the next, keeping track of the total number of throws. Try playing nine separate holes. The player who finishes the course using the *fewest* number of throws is the winner.

RATING: ⚾

PLAYERS:
2 or more

YOU NEED:
A rubber ball
for each player

Y ou can play this game almost anywhere, but wide open spaces are best. To start, choose a target that is far away. It might be a tree, a large rock or a trash can. If you can, pick something that is too far to reach with a single throw. That target is the first hole in your game.

As the game begins, each player throws the ball at the target. When the ball rolls to a stop, he picks it up and throws again. Keep track of the number of throws it takes until you hit the target with the ball.

When every player has hit the target, choose a new one for the second hole.

BALLPARK BASEBALL

BIG POCKETS

At the start of every big-league game, there are 12 dozen baseballs ready to be used. Before the game, the umpire behind home plate fills his pockets with baseballs to replace the ones that are hit into the stands and taken home as souvenirs. Others are thrown out when they are nicked or damaged. A pitcher who does not like the feel of a ball or a batter who thinks it looks dirty may ask the umpire to get rid of that ball, too.

When you're at a game, try counting the number of balls used during a single inning. Watch as they're hit into the stands or tossed out of the game. How many balls did it take to complete the inning?

TARGET PRACTICE

Before each pitch, the catcher holds up his glove as a target. The pitch-

Throw ball here!

er then tries to hit that target. The first baseman's big glove is also a target for throws from other infielders after they scoop up ground balls.

You and your friends should set targets with your glove when you play, too. Try to hit your team-mate's target with every throw you make.

AROUND THE HORN

Before each inning, a team practices its throws. When the pitcher finishes his last warm-up toss, the catcher takes the ball and throws it to second base. The infielders throw it so everyone gets one final chance to hold the ball and throw it before it goes back to the pitcher.

When you play with your friends, do the same thing. Make sure each infielder gets a chance to feel the ball one last time before the inning starts. That will help keep him ready in case the next ball comes his way.

SPINNING BALL

Watch the pitcher on the mound. As he gets ready for each pitch, he hides the ball in his glove or spins it in his hand. He does not want the other team to see how he's holding it.

That would tell the batter what type of pitch is coming.

Try this yourself. Hold a ball behind your back. Can you spin it around and around without dropping it? Now put it in your glove. Can you reach into your glove and grab it by the seams without looking?

"I do all the little things that help me throw runners out. I get to the ball fast, and I catch it out in front of me so I'm always ready to throw. When I first came up to the Twins, some teams tried to run on my arm, but I taught them not to try taking an extra base on Puck!"

Bottle Ball

Line up four bottles on a wall or a table. They should stand side to side in a row. There should be about an inch of space between the bottles.

The first batter stands about 10 feet from the bottles. She takes three throws and tries to knock down as many bottles as she can. (If knocking them down is too easy, stand a bit farther away.)

After she finishes, count the bottles. If one bottle fell, that's a single; two bottles down is a double; three is a triple; all four is a home run. Set up the bottles and throw again. A team stays at bat as long as its players knock down at least one bottle with a set of three throws. When someone misses with all three throws, the inning is over. Play a five-inning game and see who scores the most runs.

Hole in One

RATING: ⚾⚾

PLAYERS: 2

YOU NEED:
Ball, tire or hoop

Before you start, hang your target from a sturdy tree branch. The target should have a large hole in the middle. You can use a hula hoop, a life preserver or an old tire. (You may need an adult to help you hang it.)

Two players stand on opposite sides about 15 feet from the target. They try to toss the ball back and forth through the hole in the middle. Score three points each time your throw goes through the hole. Score one point if you hit the target but the ball does not go through it. The first player able to score 15 points is the winner.

Off the Wall

RATING: ⚾⚾

PLAYERS:
4 to 8

YOU NEED:
A rubber ball, a wall, chalk

Try this game in a school-yard or a playground. Use a wall without any windows.

Begin by setting up your field. Standing a few feet away, throw the ball off the wall and see where it bounces. Make a chalk line at that spot. If you don't have chalk, use a row of small pebbles to make your line.

Now choose up sides. The team that is in the field first spreads out behind the line. The other team "bats" first. Instead of hitting the ball, each batter throws it as hard as she can against the wall. If the ball bounces off the wall but does not reach the line, the batter is out. If a player catches it on a fly, the batter is also out. But if the ball bounces beyond the line, it's a hit. The batter gets one base for each bounce. Four or more bounces counts as a home run. Play using baseball rules.

In this game you need to throw the ball hard off the wall, but the throw that bounces the farthest isn't always the best. Learn to throw line drives and to aim the ball so it lands where fielders can't reach it. That will help you get on base and score runs.

THROWING RECORDS

STRIKE! Arthur "Candy" Cummings was a pitcher in the early days of baseball. He found a new way to get batters out by inventing a spinning pitch called the curveball.

STRIKE! No one knows who threw the fastest fastball of all, but it might have been Nolan Ryan. Using a radar gun, Ryan's fastball was measured at speeds just over 100 miles per hour. With the help of his fastball, Ryan struck out 5,668 batters—the most in major-league history.

BALL! Dolly Gray pitched for the Washington Senators. On one particular day, Dolly simply could not throw strikes. He walked eight batters in one inning, including seven in a row!

STRIKE! William Howard Taft never played in the big leagues, but he made one of the most famous throws of all time. On April 14, 1914, he became the first president to throw out a baseball to start a season.

STRIKE! In the 1988 season, Orel Hershiser set an incredible record. The Dodger pitcher threw 59 innings in a row without giving up a single run.

BALL! Chick Fraser pitched for 14 years in the big leagues and holds a wild record. During his career he hit 215 batters with his pitches.

STRIKE! Red Barrett was a player for the Boston Braves who made every pitch count. He pitched and won a complete game in 1944 while throwing only 58 pitches.

BALL! A spitball is a pitch that uses a ball loaded with saliva. It's not only gross—it's illegal! It wasn't always that way: In the early days of baseball many pitchers used spit, grease or tobacco juice to make a ball curve. The last pitcher to legally throw a spitter was Burleigh Grimes in 1934.

Stoop Ball

RATING: ⚾⚾⚾

PLAYERS:
2 or more

YOU NEED:
A rubber ball,
a stoop

A "stoop" is a city name for the stone steps that lead up to many homes. Stoops are a great place to sit or to play games with a soft rubber ball.

Stand about four or five feet in front of a stoop. (It's a good idea to draw a line so each player knows exactly where to stand.) Throw the ball at the stoop and try to get it to come back to you. Sometimes the ball will hit the crack at the spot where two steps meet. If it does, it will come back slowly, like a pop-up. Or it may hit the edge of the step itself. Then it bounces back quickly, like a line drive.

It takes practice to get the ball to come back to you. Flip the ball gently and don't aim it. Look at the spot where you want the ball to go. As you throw the ball and catch it, you score points:

■ *If you hit the crack between the steps and catch the ball on a fly, score 2 points.*

■ *If you hit the crack but catch it on one bounce, score 1 point.*

■ *If you hit the edge of the stoop and catch that fast-moving ball, score 10 points.*

■ *If you hit the edge and catch it on one bounce, score 5 points.*

Keep throwing and adding up points. Your turn ends when you miss the stoop or fail to catch the ball. Now the next player gives it a try. Keep taking turns and adding to your score. You must reach 100 to win the game. When a player gets to 100, he should keep going until he misses, since the other players get last licks. If more than one person goes over 100, the player with the highest score wins.

Stoop Baseball

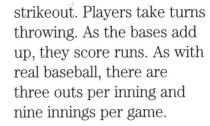

strikeout. Players take turns throwing. As the bases add up, they score runs. As with real baseball, there are three outs per inning and nine innings per game.

RATING: ◗ ◗ ◗

PLAYERS:
4 or more

YOU NEED:
A rubber ball, a stoop, chalk

This is a game for two teams. Draw a line at least 10 feet from the stoop. The team that is in the field spreads out behind that line.

The other team now bats. The first batter stands right by the stoop and throws the ball as hard as she can against it. If the ball flies over the line and into the playing field, it's a fair ball. If the fielders catch it, the batter is out. If it bounces, she gets one base for each bounce. Four or more bounces is a home run.

A player gets three tries to throw a fair ball. If she misses all three, that's a

NO-FRILLS DRILLS

DOWN THE LINE

Purpose: To work on basic throwing technique.

Players form two long lines about 20 feet apart.

The player at one end has a bucket of baseballs. He throws the first ball to the player standing across from him. She catches it and throws it back to the next player in line. The ball goes back and forth down the line in a zigzag pattern from one player to the next.

After the first ball is on its way, the first player throws another ball and then another. One by one, the balls keep going. When the last ball reaches the last player, repeat the drill in the opposite direction until all the balls are returned to the first player.

RELAY DRILL

Purpose: To develop accuracy and teamwork.

Three players work together in this drill. They stand in a straight line. The distance between them should be about the same as the distance from one base to the next.

The first player throws the ball to the second one, who spins as if he were making a relay throw. He fires the ball to the other player, who catches it and pretends she is tagging out a runner coming to her base. Repeat this drill with the ball going from the last player back to the first. Switch positions now and then so each player spends time in the middle.

BASE DRILL

Purpose: To practice throws used in game situations.

This is a good drill for outfielders getting ready to play a game. One player throws the ball to each outfielder, who works on getting in position to make strong, accurate throws, as if runners were heading to certain bases. Here's how it goes:

■ The left fielder makes two throws to third base and two more to home plate.

■ The center fielder throws two to second base and two to home plate.

■ The right fielder throws two to third and two to home.

As you go through this drill, make it as much like a real game as possible. After each throw, the infielder or catcher who gets the ball should turn and make a tag as if a runner were sliding into the base.

LONG TOSS DRILL

Purpose: To build arm strength for long throws.

Stand in the outfield, about 25 feet away from another player. Begin tossing the ball back and forth. At first, throw easy fly balls that stretch your shoulder muscles. As the drill continues, step back each time you catch the ball. As you step back, the throws will get longer. Start to work on throwing lower until you're throwing line drives to each other. Concentrate on making accurate throws. When you can no longer reach the other player on a fly, try making accurate one-bounce throws.

KIRBY PUCKETT

KIRBY'S TIPS

1. Never aim when you throw or pitch. Just look where you want the ball to go and let your arm do the rest.

2. Practice your throwing motion so you throw or pitch the ball the same way each time. Always throw with high, easy tosses so your muscles can stretch out and get loose.

3. Don't throw the ball too hard or try any fancy pitches. You might end up with an aching arm.

Last Licks

N ow that you can hit, run, throw, and catch, you are ready to play baseball. The skills you learned will help you play other sports, too. Here are a few final baseball tips and some games that pull it all together, whether you're a rookie or an all-star.

KEEPING SCORE

There is more to keeping score than knowing how many runs each team has. Some baseball coaches and fans keep a record called a scorecard. It tells them what happened every time a player came to bat. Each at-bat is recorded in a small box, using symbols to fit a lot of information in a little space. Together, all the boxes tell the story of what happened in a game.

Every position on the field is represented by a number, starting with the pitcher. Here's how it goes:

1 = PITCHER
2 = CATCHER
3 = FIRST BASEMAN
4 = SECOND BASEMAN
5 = THIRD BASEMAN
6 = SHORTSTOP
7 = LEFT FIELDER
8 = CENTER FIELDER
9 = RIGHT FIELDER

There are also ways to describe most of the things that happen on a play. Here are some typical symbols you can use:

BB = WALK
K = STRIKEOUT
1B = SINGLE
2B = DOUBLE
3B = TRIPLE
HR = HOME RUN
E = ERROR
SB = STOLEN BASE
FC = FIELDER'S CHOICE
DP = DOUBLE PLAY

To set up your scorecard, write the batting lineup for each team. Now, as players hit, use your symbols to tell the story of the game. For instance:

■ The first batter hits a ground ball. The shortstop catches it and throws the batter out at first base. Find that batter on your scorecard. In his first inning box write **6-3**.

■ The next batter walks. In his box, start to make a baseball diamond. Draw the

line from home plate to first base to show where he went. In the corner, write **BB** to explain how he got there.

■ The next batter hits a home run. Make the whole baseball diamond in his box and write **HR**. Go back to the batter before him and finish his baseball diamond. That shows that he scored, too.

■ Keep your record going from inning to inning. Don't be afraid to add your own symbols, too. For instance, if the left fielder caught a fly ball, you would write **7**. If he made a great catch, you could write **7!** instead.

■ During a game you can use your scorecard to see how players are doing from one at-bat to the next. At the end you'll have your own play-by-play account of your day at the ballpark.

THE PERFECT POSITION

When you start out playing baseball, it's a good idea to try as many positions as possible. You can take advantage of different skills as you move around the field. Excellent defensive players are often found at shortstop, second base and center field. Big hitters settle in at first base, third base, left field and right field. The best all-around player on a young team is often the pitcher. This chart can help you think about where to play, but remember, it's only a guide. Don't be afraid to try any position you want.

CHECK YOUR STRENGTHS

POSITION	STRONG ARM	LOTS OF ACTION	MUST TAKE CHARGE	MUST RUN FAST	GOOD FOR LEFTIES?
Pitcher	YES	YES	YES	NO	YES
Catcher	YES	YES	YES	NO	NO
First base	NO	YES	NO	NO	YES
Second base	NO	YES	NO	YES	NO
Third base	YES	NO	NO	NO	NO
Shortstop	YES	YES	YES	YES	NO
Left field	NO	NO	NO	NO	YES
Right field	YES	NO	NO	NO	YES
Center field	YES	YES	YES	YES	YES

Bounce Baseball

RATING: ◍

PLAYERS:
2 full teams

YOU NEED:
A rubber ball or
tennis ball

Hitting a base-
ball can be
hard, so here's a way
to play a whole baseball
game without hitting. In
fact, in this game you don't
even use a bat. Instead,
play with a ball that has lots
of bounce to it.

Choose sides and set up
a field as if you were playing regular baseball. Now
the first player
"bats." He steps
up to home plate with the
ball in his hand. The batter
throws the ball so that it
bounces off home plate.
While the fielders chase the
ball, he runs to first.

All the regular rules of
baseball apply. The team
that scores the most runs
wins the game.

Three-Box Baseball

This is a game for two players. Play it on a sidewalk where there are three even squares, or use chalk to make three boxes on any smooth pavement.

The two players stand on opposite sides of the three-box field. Players must keep one foot behind the box at all times. They can move the other foot up along the side of the box, but they cannot step inside it.

One player takes the field. With an underhand toss, she pitches the ball into the box closest to the player who is batting. If she misses the box, that is a walk for the first batter. If the ball bounces in the box, her opponent slaps at it. He must hit it into the box that is closest to her.

■ **If the ball bounces in that box, it's a hit.** Count one base for every bounce. (Only the first bounce must be in the box.)

■ **If the fielder drops the ball, the batter is safe on an error.** Again, he gets a base for every bounce.

■ **If the batter misses the box or the fielder catches the ball before it bounces, the batter is out.**

As the game continues, move your imaginary players around the bases and score runs. Play a nine-inning game to see who wins.

Danish Rounders

DOWN

RATING: ⚾⚾⚾

PLAYERS:
Two teams

YOU NEED:
Bat, ball, bases
and gloves

Before there was baseball, people played a game called rounders. Try this modern version of the game. Any number can play, but it works best with lots of players on each team.

To begin, one team takes the field. The other team lines up in the order that they will bat at the start of the inning.

At the start, rounders looks just like baseball. The batter swings, hits the ball and runs to first base. If the ball is caught on a fly, the batter is out. If not, the fielder throws it to the *pitcher* who picks it up. When she gets it, she throws the ball on the ground and shouts "Down!" If the runner is not standing on a base at that moment, he is out.

The players take their turns batting, but they run the bases in a different way than they do in baseball. A runner is *not* forced to leave a base, so lots of runners can be on one base at the same time.

The fielders keep making plays and throwing the ball to the pitcher. Whenever she shouts "Down!", any runner who is not standing safely on a base is out. Every time a runner crosses home plate, his team scores a run. He goes to the end of the line to wait his next turn to hit. Batters who are called out also join the end of the line, so the batting order changes as the inning continues.

Sometimes a team has all its players on the bases and no one left to hit. When that happens, the last player to bat comes back to home plate and hits one more time. If his team can score a runner, the inning continues. If they cannot, his team takes the field.

As in baseball, the team with the highest score after nine innings is the winner.

A GAME OF NUMBERS

In the old days, players did not wear numbers. Now teams use numbers and even names to help fans know who's who.

The first major-league team to wear numbers was the New York Yankees. They took their batting order and numbered the players from 1 to 9. For instance, Babe Ruth batted third. From that day on, the Babe wore #3 no matter where he batted in the lineup.

Certain numbers seem to be particularly popular. Once a great player wears it, others who think of him as an idol want to wear it, too. Willie Mays wore 24 before Ken Griffey Jr. did. After Hank Aaron wore 44, sluggers like Reggie Jackson did, too.

When you wear a uniform, you can pick any number as long as no other player on the team has it. Pick your birthday, your lucky number or your favorite player's number.

"When I came up to the Twins, I wanted to wear number 14. That was Ernie Banks' number, and he was always my idol. But Kent Hrbek had that number already. My next choice was 24 for Willie Mays, but Tom Brunansky had that one. So I ended up with 34. To tell you the truth, I was so happy to be there that any number would do!"

KIRBY'S LAST LICKS

1. Be inquisitive! Don't be afraid to ask questions. Believe me, you're never too old to discover things that will make you a better player.

2. Be positive! You may not be the best player, but that's okay. Do the little things that help your team.

3. Be happy! Don't worry about mistakes. Learn from them and put them behind you. Baseball is meant to be enjoyed, so play the game and have fun!

Index

How many outs?

Where will the batter hit the ball?

Where do I throw if the ball is hit to me?

C

D

E,F

G,H